D0176940

COULD A WALRUS PLAY THE SAXOPHONE?

And Other Questions About Animals

Paul Mason

Raintree

Raintree is an imprint of Capstone Global Library Limited, a company incorporated in England and Wales having its registered office at 7 Pilgrim Street, London, EC4V 6LB – Registered company number: 6695582

www.raintreepublishers.co.uk
myorders@raintreepublishers.co.uk

Text © Capstone Global Library Limited 2014
First published in hardback in 2014
Paperback edition first published in 2015
The moral rights of the proprietor have been asserted.

Edited by Dan Nunn, Rebecca Rissman, and John-Paul Wilkins
Designed by Steve Mead
Picture research by Mica Brancic
Production by Sophia Argyris
Originated by Capstone Global Library Ltd
Printed and bound in China by CTPS

ISBN 978 1 406 25946 9 (hardback)
17 16 15 14 13
10 9 8 7 6 5 4 3 2 1

ISBN 978 1 406 25952 0 (paperback)
18 17 16 15 14
10 9 8 7 6 5 4 3 2 1

British Library Cataloguing in Publication Data
Mason, Paul.
Could a walrus play the saxophone? and other questions about animals. -- (Questions you never thought you'd ask)

A full catalogue record for this book is available from the British Library.

Acknowledgements

We would like to thank the following for permission to reproduce photographs: Getty Images pp. 7 (Gallo Images/Federico Veronesi), 9 (Flickr/© 2006 Sean McCann), 23 (Peter Arnold/Jeffrey L. Rotman); Science Photo Library p. 21 (Visuals Unlimited, Inc./ Eric Tourneret); Shutterstock pp. 4 orchestra (© Ferenc Szelepcsenyi), 4 walrus (© ericlefrancais), 4 saxophone (© kuznetcov_konstantin), 5 walrus (© yui), 5 saxophone (© kuznetcov_konstantin), 6 (© jorisvo), 8 earwig (© Scott Hussey), 8 lady's ear (© Tatjana Romanova), 10 man in swimming gear (© Lilyana Vynogradova), 10 water background (© Clover), 10 medusa (© Jiri Vaclavek), 11 man in swimming gear (© Lilyana Vynogradova), 11 toilet (© Jiri Hera), 11 plastic bucket (© Andrey Eremin), 12 cow (© Dudarev Mikhail), 12 bomb explosion (© James Thew), 13 (© majeczka), 14 (© wtamas), 15 earthworm (© D. Kucharski & K. Kucharska), 15 soil background (© PhotoHouse), 16 detective with magnifying glass (© Richard Peterson), 16 green plastic plate with crumbs (© Jaimie Duplass), 16 bloodhound dog (© Susan Schmitz), 16 wooden table (© MaxPhotographer), 17 (© Jostein Hauge), 18 witch (© Fer Gregory), 18 toad (© alexsvirid), 19 toad (© Angelo Giampiccolo), 19 male hand (© hans.slegers), 20 cow (© arniep), 20 map (© Atlaspix), 20 weather symbols (© mesimply), 22 lemon shark (© FAUP), 22 hypnotic whirlpool eye (© Biczó Zsolt), 22 silver pocket watch (© Graça Victoria), 22 water background (© Clover), 24 (© Daniel Alvarez), 25 (© Bridgena Barnard), 26 (© Matej Kastelic), 27 red sports car (© Charlie Hutton), 27 skittles (© Becky Stares), 27 bull (© Vera Zinkova), 27 coloured footballs (© Perry Correll), 28 goldfish (© dibrova), 28 gameshow host (© criben), 29 (© Richard Peterson).

Cover photographs of walrus (© Nejron Photo) and saxophone (© kuznetcov_konstantin) reproduced with permission of Shutterstock.

We would like to thank Diana Bentley and Marla Conn for their invaluable help in the preparation of this book.

Every effort has been made to contact copyright holders of any material reproduced in this book. Any omissions will be rectified in subsequent printings if notice is given to the publisher.

Disclaimer
All the internet addresses (URLs) given in this book were valid at the time of going to press. However, due to the dynamic nature of the internet, some addresses may have changed, or sites may have changed or ceased to exist since publication. While the author and publisher regret any inconvenience this may cause readers, no responsibility for any such changes can be accepted by either the author or the publisher.

CONTENTS

Could a walrus play the saxophone? 4

What are crocodile tears? 6

Could an earwig crawl into your ear? 8

Can you cure a jellyfish sting by weeing on it? 10

Could cows really destroy the world?......................12

Does cutting a worm in half make two worms? 14

Do dogs leave fingerprints? 16

Can you catch warts from a toad? 18

Can cows forecast the weather?................................20

Can you hypnotize a shark? 22

Do hyenas really laugh?..24

Does red really make bulls angry?............................26

Do goldfish really have bad memories?....................28

Glossary..30

Find out more..31

Index..32

Some words are shown in bold, **like this**. You can find out what they mean by looking in the glossary.

COULD A WALRUS PLAY THE SAXOPHONE?

If you visited the zoo in Istanbul, Turkey, you might think the answer was "yes". Sara the walrus appears with her saxophone and puts it in her mouth. The music quickly starts.

Sadly, walruses aren't equipped to play the saxophone in real life. Sara is just **miming**. The music actually comes from a sound system!

Big flippers + tiny buttons = impossible to play notes!

WHAT ARE CROCODILE TEARS?

Crocodiles do not cry because they are sad! The crying actually happens when they eat. This is because crocodiles cannot chew. They have to swallow their food in big chunks. Gulping down these chunks forces **fluid** from **glands** around their eyes.

BOO HOO!

A crocodile's tears are difficult to spot because they are always soaking wet!

COULD AN EARWIG CRAWL INTO YOUR EAR?

Even medical books used to say that earwigs sometimes crawled into people's ears. Earwigs do like warm, moist places. Fortunately, though, these places do *not* include human ears!

Did you know?
Although earwigs have wings, they hardly ever fly.

Earwigs were named because of the shape of their wings. When stretched out, they look like human ears.

CAN YOU CURE A JELLYFISH STING BY WEEING ON IT?

Jellyfish stings happen when a jellyfish leaves tiny stingers in your skin. These contain **venom**. Washing jellyfish stings down with wee is said to **cure** them. In fact, it will probably make the stingers release *extra* venom. Ow!

Some experts say the best way to treat most jellyfish stings is to wash them down with saltwater.

saltwater

✓

wee

COULD COWS REALLY DESTROY THE WORLD?

Have cows perhaps developed a super bomb to blow us all up? No! It's cow farts people worry about. Cow farts are said to contain gases that cause **global warming** to get worse.

MOOOO!

This is wrong, of course. It's cow burps, not farts, which could destroy the world!

cow fart does little harm

cow burp contains gas that is terrible for the environment

DOES CUTTING A WORM IN HALF MAKE TWO WORMS?

No. If you accidentally cut a garden worm in two, the best result would be:
- one shorter worm
- one dead bit of worm.

A worm can only survive being cut in two if it happens near its tail. If you cut it in the middle, both parts would wriggle as if they were alive. Then they would die.

DO DOGS LEAVE FINGERPRINTS?

No – but if you think Fido's been stealing your biscuits, there might be another way to find out. Each dog's nose print is as **unique** as a human fingerprint.

"It wasn't me... honest!"

CAN YOU CATCH WARTS FROM A TOAD?

Toads do *look* warty. It's no wonder people used to think they could catch **warts** from them. In fact, the lumps and bumps on a toad's skin aren't warts at all. They are **glands**. When a toad is scared, the glands release a slimy liquid called mucus. Some toads can even release poison!

CAN COWS FORECAST THE WEATHER?

It's claimed that cows lie down when they sense rain is on its way. This is not true, though. Cows actually lie down after eating food.

And now for the weather ...

Did you know?

Some animals do seem to be able to **predict** storms:

- Sharks head for deep water
- Birds go to their nests
- Bees shelter in their **hives**

CAN YOU HYPNOTIZE A SHARK?

Sharks are feared around the world. But some sharks can be **hypnotized** – just by rubbing the tip of their nose! Even deadly killers such as the great white shark can be affected.

How to hypnotize a shark

Step 1. Rub shark's nose
Step 2. Stand shark on head
Step 3. Rub nose more

Shark is hypnotized
for 15 minutes!

Did you know?
In 1997, a killer whale
was seen hypnotizing
a great white shark –
which it then ate!

DO HYENAS REALLY LAUGH?

Hyenas crunch through bone with their powerful jaws. They can run faster than a man. They're so nasty, people even say hyenas laugh when they kill something. This is not actually true, though. The noise *sounds* like laughter to us. But it's just one hyena telling another that it can eat first.

Ha! Ha!

DOES RED REALLY MAKE BULLS ANGRY?

There's an old saying that something that makes you angry is, "like a red rag to a bull". In fact, bulls may not even see red. They are quite likely to confuse it with blue or green.

Is it the red **cape** making this bull angry – or the man sticking hooks in him?

DO GOLDFISH REALLY HAVE BAD MEMORIES?

Goldfish are said to have 3-second memories. In fact, they are quite good at remembering things. Goldfish have been taught to fetch objects and other tricks. They even remember the tricks months later.

What is the capital of France?

Umm...

Did you know?
Elephants have great memories. They can recognize old friends from years ago.

Hello old friend! Haven't seen you for ages...

GLOSSARY

cape sleeveless coat that does up around the neck and hangs down around your body

cure make someone who is unwell better

fluid liquid without a fixed shape, such as water

gland part of an animal that releases liquid

global warming increase in Earth's temperature. Global warming is responsible for changes in our weather and more natural disasters.

hive place where bees live

hypnotize put into a dreamy state of mind, in which you do not act for yourself

miming pretending you are doing something, but without actually doing it

predict say what will happen in the future

unique one of a kind

venom substance that is harmful when injected under the skin

wart small, hard lump on the skin

FIND OUT MORE

Books

Animal Top Tens series, Anita Ganeri (Raintree, 2009)

Animals: A Children's Encyclopedia (Dorling Kindersley, 2008)

Wild Animal Atlas (National Geographic Kids, 2010)

You Swallow Spiders In Your Sleep! The Fact or Fiction Behind Animals (Truth or Busted), Paul Mason (Wayland, 2012)

Websites

www.kidsbiology.com/animals-for-children.php
There are hundreds of different animals to discover on this website.

kids.nationalgeographic.com/kids/animals/creaturefeature
This website allows you to find out more about your favourite animals.

INDEX

bees 21
birds 21
brains 17
bulls 26–27
burps 13

cows 12–13, 20
crocodile tears
  6–7
cutting worms in
  half 14–15

dogs 16–17

ears 8, 9
earwigs 8–9
elephants 29

farts 12, 13
fingerprints 16
fluids 6, 30

gases 12, 13
glands 6, 18, 19,
  30

global warming
  12, 30
goldfish 28

hives 21, 30
hyenas 24–25
hypnotize 22–23,
  30

jellyfish stings
  10–11

killer whales 23

laughter 24

memories 28–29
miming 4, 30
mucus 18

nose prints 16, 17

poison 10, 18
predict 21, 30

red colour 26

saltwater 11
saxophone 4–5
sharks 21, 22–23
storms 21

toads 18–19

unique 16, 30

venom 10, 30

walruses 4–5
warts 18, 30
weather
  forecasting
  20–21
wee 10, 11
worms 14–15